KUMON®
MATH. READING. SUCCESS.

What is Kumon?

Kumon is the world's largest supplemental education provider and a leader in producing outstanding results. After-school programs in math and reading at Kumon Centers around the globe have been helping children succeed for 50 years.

Kumon Workbooks represent just a fraction of our complete curriculum of preschool-to-college-level material assigned at Kumon Centers under the supervision of trained Kumon Instructors.

The Kumon Method enables each child to progress successfully by practicing material until concepts are mastered and advancing in small, manageable increments. Instructors carefully assign materials and pace advancement according to the strengths and needs of each individual student.

Students usually attend a Kumon Center twice a week and practice at home the other five days. Assignments take about twenty minutes.

Kumon helps students of all ages and abilities master the basics, improve concentration and study habits, and build confidence.

How did Kumon begin?

IT ALL BEGAN IN JAPAN 50 YEARS AGO when a parent and teacher named Toru Kumon found a way to help his son Takeshi do better in school. At the prompting of his wife, he created a series of short assignments that his son could complete successfully in less than 20 minutes a day and that would ultimately make high school math easy. Because each was just a bit more challenging than the last, Takeshi was able to master the skills and gain the confidence to keep advancing.

This unique self-learning method was so successful that Toru's son was able to do calculus by the time he was in the sixth grade. Understanding the value of good reading comprehension, Mr. Kumon then developed a reading program employing the same method. His programs are the basis and inspiration of those offered at Kumon Centers today under the expert guidance of professional Kumon Instructors.

Mr. Toru Kumon
Founder of Kumon

What can Kumon do for my child?

Kumon is geared to children of all ages and skill levels. Whether you want to give your child a leg up in his or her schooling, build a strong foundation for future studies or address a possible learning problem, Kumon provides an effective program for developing key learning skills given the strengths and needs of each individual child.

What makes Kumon so different?

Kumon uses neither a classroom model nor a tutoring approach. It's designed to facilitate self-acquisition of the skills and study habits needed to improve academic performance. This empowers children to succeed on their own, giving them a sense of accomplishment that fosters further achievement. Whether for remedial work or enrichment, a child advances according to individual ability and initiative to reach his or her full potential. Kumon is not only effective, but also surprisingly affordable.

What is the role of the Kumon Instructor?

Kumon Instructors regard themselves more as mentors or coaches than teachers in the traditional sense. Their principal role is to provide the direction, support and encouragement that will guide the student to performing at 100% of his or her potential. Along with their rigorous training in the Kumon Method, all Kumon Instructors share a passion for education and an earnest desire to help children succeed.

KUMON FOSTERS:

- A mastery of the basics of reading and math
- Improved concentration and study habits
- Increased self-discipline and self-confidence
- A proficiency in material at every level
- Performance to each student's full potential
- A sense of accomplishment

▶▶ GETTING STARTED IS EASY. Just call us at 877.586.6671 or visit kumon.com to request our free brochure and find a Kumon Center near you. We'll direct you to an Instructor who will be happy to speak with you about how Kumon can address your child's particular needs and arrange a free placement test. There are more than 1,700 Kumon Centers in the U.S. and Canada, and students may enroll at any time throughout the year, even summer. Contact us today.

FIND OUT MORE ABOUT KUMON MATH & READING CENTERS.
Receive a free copy of our parent guide, *Every Child an Achiever,* by visiting
kumon.com/go.survey or calling 877.586.6671

Name

Date

To parents
On the following pages, your child will learn adjectives paired with their opposites. If your child encounters difficulty, explain that adjectives help describe things and ask about the difference between each picture.

■ An adjective is a word that describes a noun. A noun is a person, place, or thing. Look at each picture and say each adjective and noun aloud. Then trace and write the words below.

big dog   small dog

big dog   small dog

big dog   small dog

big dog   small dog

big dog   small dog

big dog   small dog

■ Look at each picture and say each adjective and noun aloud.
  Then trace and write the words below.

big dog

big dog

small dog

small dog

big cat

big cat

small cat

small cat

2 Practicing Sentences
Using big and small

Name

Date

To parents
In this activity, your child will learn to use adjectives in a short sentence. If your child is having trouble reading a sentence, ask him or her to describe the picture next to it.

■ Look at each picture and say each sentence aloud.
  Then trace the sentences below.

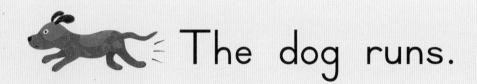 The dog runs.

The big dog runs.

The big dog runs.

The big dog runs.

The small dog runs.

The small dog runs.

The small dog runs.

■ Look at each picture and say each sentence aloud.
  Then trace and write the sentences below.

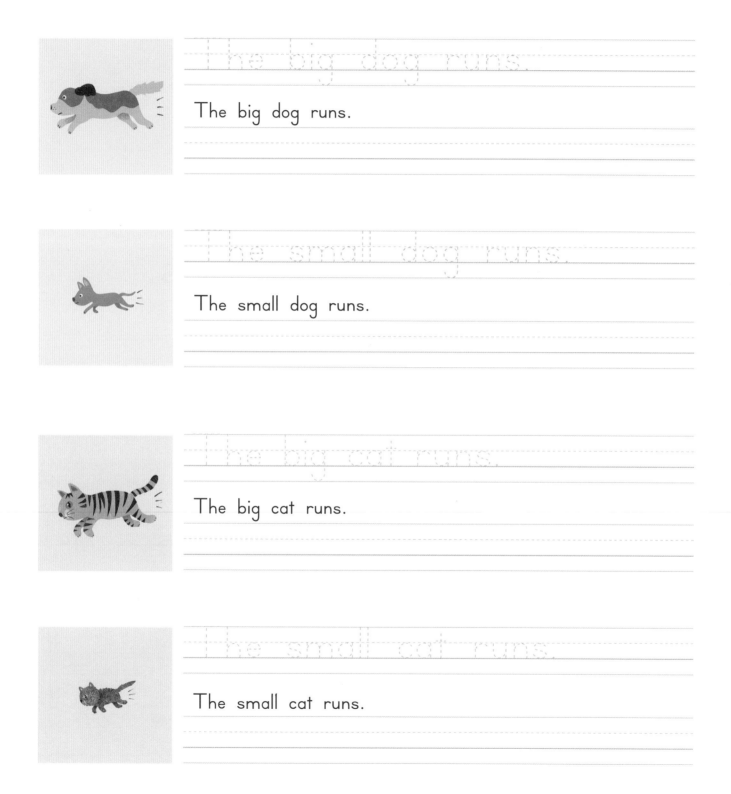

The big dog runs.

The big dog runs.

The small dog runs.

The small dog runs.

The big cat runs.

The big cat runs.

The small cat runs.

The small cat runs.

Name

Date

■ Look at each picture and say each adjective and noun aloud.
   Then trace and write the words below.

old man

young man

old man

young man

old man

young man

old man

young man

old man

young man

■ Look at each picture and say each adjective and noun aloud.
  Then trace and write the words below.

old man

young man

old lady

young lady

Practicing Sentences
Using old and young

Name	
Date	

■ Look at each picture and say each sentence aloud.
  Then trace the sentences below.

 The man eats.

 The old man eats.

The old man eats.

The old man eats.

The young man eats.

The young man eats.

The young man eats.

■ Look at each picture and say each sentence aloud.
Then trace and write the sentences below.

The old man eats.

The young man eats.

The old lady eats.

The young lady eats.

Review
Using adjectives

Name	
Date	

■ Look at each picture and say each sentence aloud.
  Then trace and write the sentences below.

The big dog runs.

The big dog runs.

The small dog runs.

The small dog runs.

The big cat runs.

The big cat runs.

The small cat runs.

The small cat runs.

■ Look at each picture and say each sentence aloud.
   Then trace and write the sentences below.

The old man eats.

The young man eats.

The old lady eats.

The young lady eats.

6 Practicing Adjectives
long and short

Name
Date

■ Look at each picture and say each adjective and noun aloud.
Then trace and write the words below.

long fish

short fish

long fish

short fish

■ Look at each picture and say each adjective and noun aloud.
   Then trace and write the words below.

long fish

short fish

long snake

short snake

7 Practicing Sentences
Using long and short

Name

Date

■ Look at each picture and say each sentence aloud.
  Then trace the sentences below.

The fish swims.

The long fish swims.

The long fish swims.

The long fish swims.

The short fish swims.

The short fish swims.

The short fish swims.

■ Look at each picture and say each sentence aloud.
   Then trace and write the sentences below.

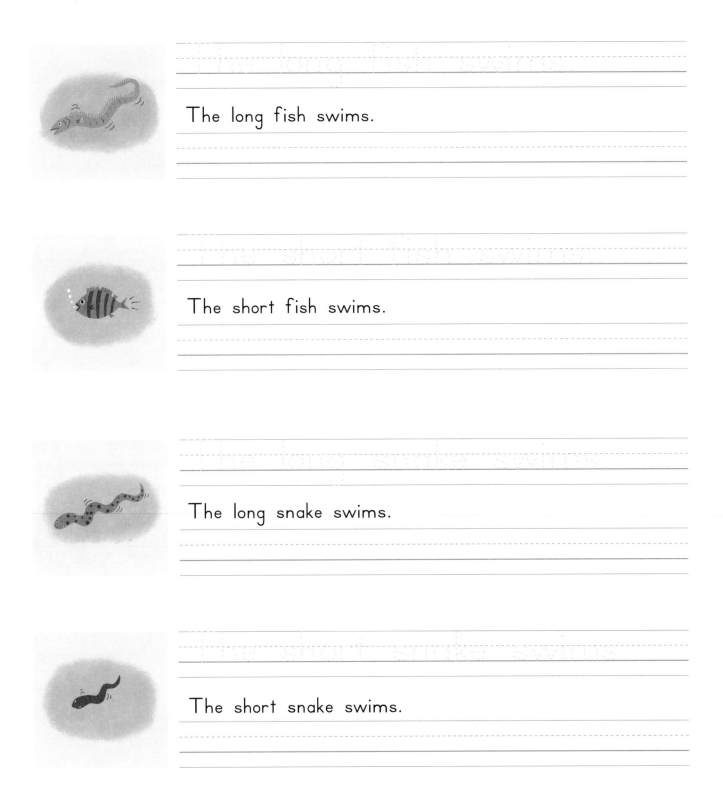

The long fish swims.

The short fish swims.

The long snake swims.

The short snake swims.

Practicing Adjectives
heavy and light

Name

Date

■ Look at each picture and say each adjective and noun aloud.
 Then trace and write the words below.

heavy frog

light frog

heavy frog

light frog

heavy frog

light frog

■ Look at each picture and say each adjective and noun aloud.
   Then trace and write the words below.

heavy frog

light frog

heavy rabbit

light rabbit

9 Practicing Sentences
Using heavy and light

Name
Date

■ Look at each picture and say each sentence aloud.
  Then trace the sentences below.

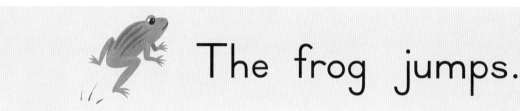

The frog jumps.

The heavy frog jumps.

The heavy frog jumps.

The heavy frog jumps.

The light frog jumps.

The light frog jumps.

The light frog jumps.

■ Look at each picture and say each sentence aloud.
   Then trace and write the sentences below.

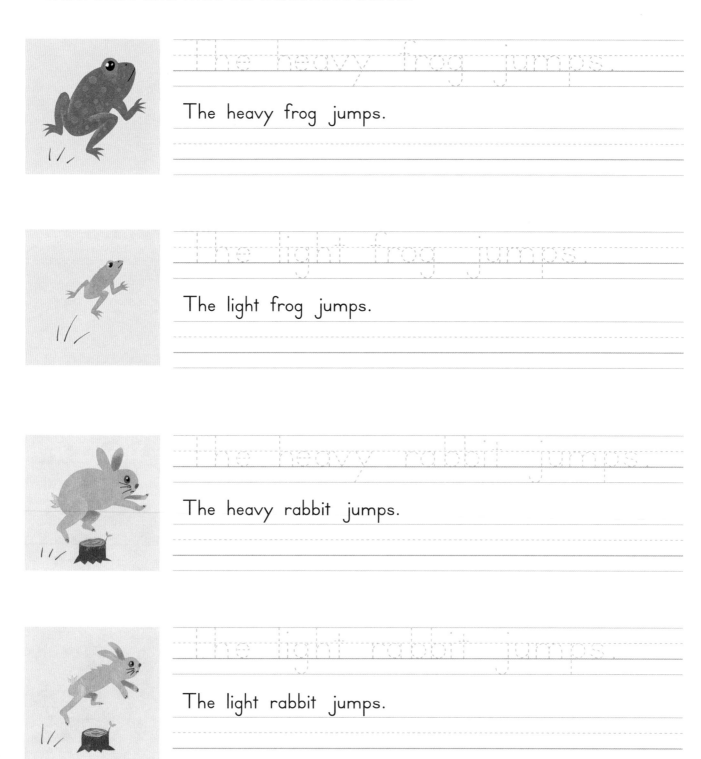

The heavy frog jumps.

The light frog jumps.

The heavy rabbit jumps.

The light rabbit jumps.

10 Review
Using adjectives

Name

Date

■ Look at each picture and say each sentence aloud.
  Then trace and write the sentences below.

The long fish swims.

The short fish swims.

The long snake swims.

The short snake swims.

■ Look at each picture and say each sentence aloud.
Then trace and write the sentences below.

The heavy frog jumps.

The heavy frog jumps.

The light frog jumps.

The light frog jumps.

The heavy rabbit jumps.

The heavy rabbit jumps.

The light rabbit jumps.

The light rabbit jumps.

11 **Practicing Adjectives**
clean and dirty

Name

Date

■ Look at each picture and say each adjective and noun aloud.
   Then trace and write the words below.

clean car   dirty car

clean car   dirty car

clean car   dirty car

clean car   dirty car

clean car   dirty car

■ Look at each picture and say each adjective and noun aloud.
  Then trace and write the words below.

clean car

dirty car

clean bike

dirty bike

Practicing Sentences
Using clean and dirty

Name

Date

■ Look at each picture and say each sentence aloud.
   Then trace the sentences below.

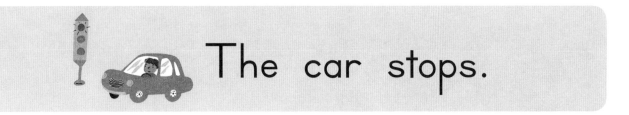

The car stops.

The clean car stops.

The clean car stops.

The clean car stops.

The dirty car stops.

The dirty car stops.

The dirty car stops.

■ Look at each picture and say each sentence aloud.
   Then trace and write the sentences below.

The clean car stops.

The dirty car stops.

The clean bike stops.

The dirty bike stops.

13 Practicing Adjectives
happy and sad

■ Look at each picture and say each adjective and noun aloud.
Then trace and write the words below.

happy boy

sad boy

happy boy

sad boy

happy boy

sad boy

happy boy

sad boy

happy boy

sad boy

■ Look at each picture and say each adjective and noun aloud.
  Then trace and write the words below.

happy boy

sad boy

happy girl

sad girl

Practicing Sentences
Using happy and sad

Name

Date

■ Look at each picture and say each sentence aloud.
  Then trace the sentences below.

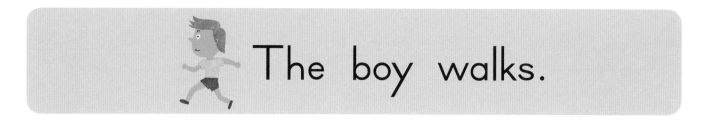

The boy walks.

The happy boy walks.

The happy boy walks.

The happy boy walks.

The sad boy walks.

The sad boy walks.

The sad boy walks.

■ Look at each picture and say each sentence aloud.
Then trace and write the sentences below.

The happy boy walks.

The sad boy walks.

The happy girl walks.

The sad girl walks.

Name
Date

■ Look at each picture and say each sentence aloud.
   Then trace and write the sentences below.

The clean car stops.

The dirty car stops.

The clean bike stops.

The dirty bike stops.

■ Look at each picture and say each sentence aloud.
   Then trace and write the sentences below.

The happy boy walks.

The sad boy walks.

The happy girl walks.

The sad girl walks.

Name

Date

■ Look at each picture and say each sentence aloud.
  Then write the sentences below.

 The big dog runs.

 The clean car stops.

 The heavy frog jumps.

 The small dog runs.

 The dirty car stops.

 The light frog jumps.

■ Look at each picture and say each sentence aloud.
  Then write the sentences below.

The big cat runs.

The clean bike stops.

The heavy rabbit jumps.

The small cat runs.

The dirty bike stops.

The light rabbit jumps.

17 Review
Using adjectives

Name
Date

■ Look at each picture and say each sentence aloud.
Then write the sentences below.

The old man eats.

The happy boy walks.

The long fish swims.

The young man eats.

The sad boy walks.

The short fish swims.

■ Look at each picture and say each sentence aloud.
 Then write the sentences below.

The old lady eats.

The happy girl walks.

The long snake swims.

The young lady eats.

The sad girl walks.

The short snake swims.

18 Practicing Sentences
Using big and small

Name

Date

To parents
Now your child will begin to learn a new sentence structure. If your child encounters difficulty, try asking them to describe the picture.

■ Look at each picture and say each sentence aloud.
   Then trace the sentences below.

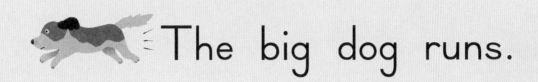

The big dog runs.

The dog is big.

The dog is big.
The dog is big.

The dog is small.

The dog is small.
The dog is small.

■ Look at each picture and say each sentence aloud.
   Then trace and write the sentences below.

The bear is big.

The bear is small.

The gorilla is big.

The gorilla is small.

Practicing Sentences
Using new and old

Name	
Date	

■ Look at each picture and say each sentence aloud.
   Then trace the sentences below.

The new ball rolls.

The ball is new.

The ball is new.

The ball is new.

The ball is old.

The ball is old.

The ball is old.

■ Look at each picture and say each sentence aloud.
  Then trace and write the sentences below.

The pen is new.

The pen is new.

The pen is old.

The pen is old.

The doll is new.

The doll is new.

The doll is old.

The doll is old.

20 Practicing Sentences
Using thin and thick

Name	
Date	

■ Look at each picture and say each sentence aloud.
  Then trace the sentences below.

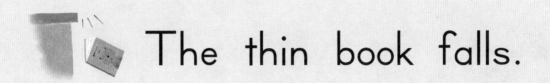

The thin book falls.

The book is thin.

The book is thin.

The book is thin.

The book is thick.

The book is thick.

The book is thick.

■ Look at each picture and say each sentence aloud.
  Then trace and write the sentences below.

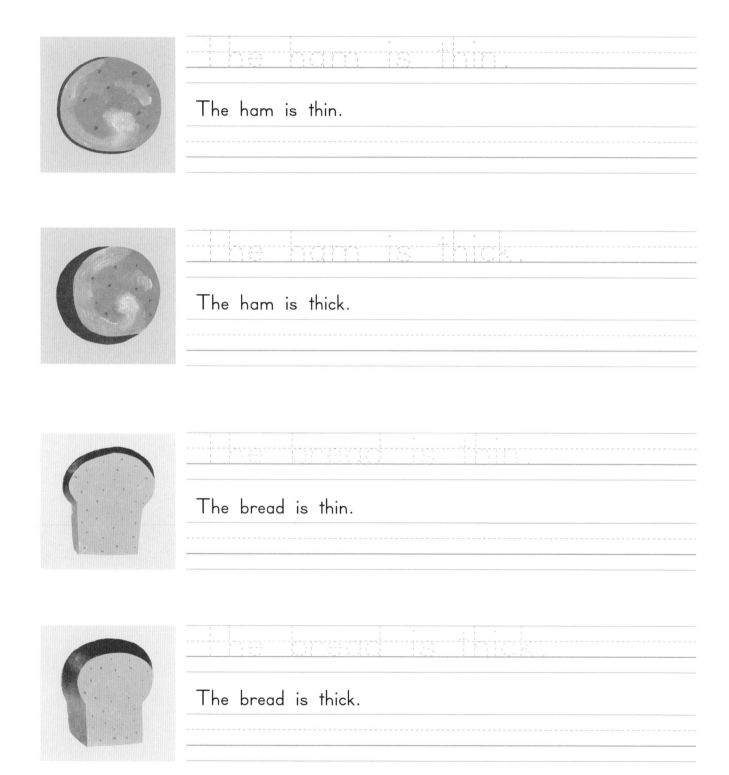

The ham is thin.

The ham is thick.

The bread is thin.

The bread is thick.

Review
Using adjectives

Name
Date

■ Look at each picture and say each sentence aloud.
  Then write the sentences below.

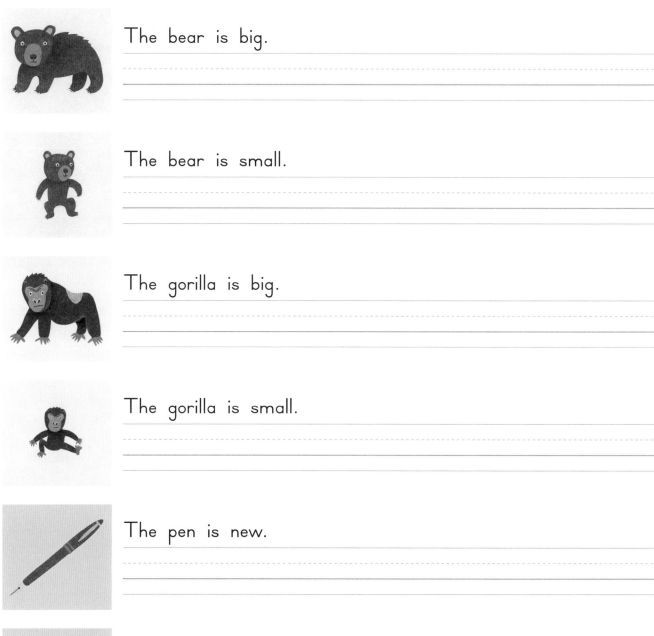

The bear is big.

The bear is small.

The gorilla is big.

The gorilla is small.

The pen is new.

The pen is old.

■ Look at each picture and say each sentence aloud.
Then write the sentences below.

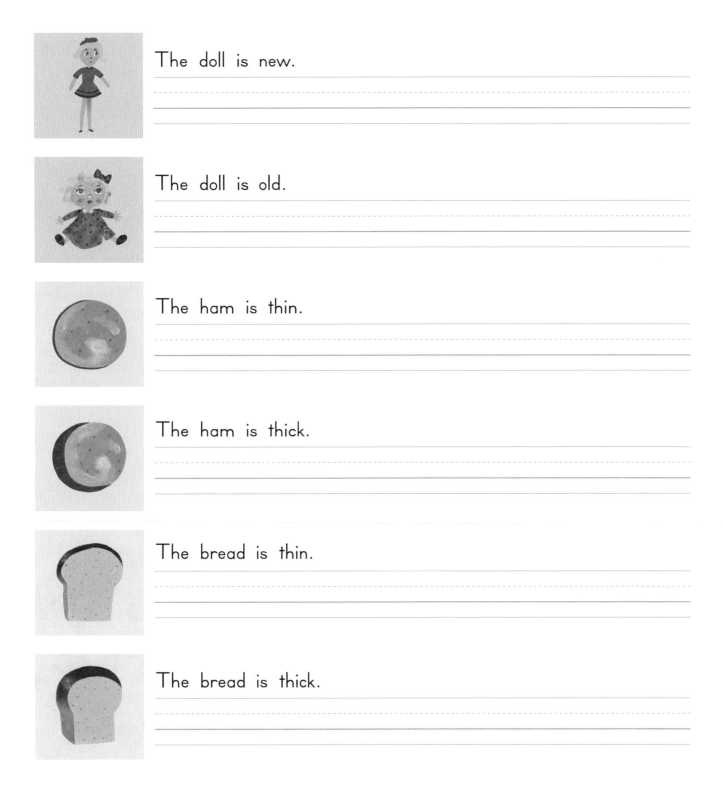

The doll is new.

The doll is old.

The ham is thin.

The ham is thick.

The bread is thin.

The bread is thick.

Practicing Sentences
Using slow and fast

Name

Date

■ Look at each picture and say each sentence aloud.
  Then trace the sentences below.

The slow horse walks.

The horse is slow.

The horse is slow.

The horse is slow.

The horse is fast.

The horse is fast.

The horse is fast.

■ Look at each picture and say each sentence aloud.
   Then trace and write the sentences below.

The truck is slow.

The truck is fast.

The zebra is slow.

The zebra is fast.

23 Practicing Sentences
Using hot and cold

Name
Date

■ Look at each picture and say each sentence aloud.
   Then trace the sentences below.

The hot milk boils.

The milk is hot.

The milk is hot.

The milk is hot.

The milk is cold.

The milk is cold.

The milk is cold.

■ Look at each picture and say each sentence aloud.
  Then trace and write the sentences below.

The tea is hot.

The tea is cold.

The soup is hot.

The soup is cold.

Practicing Sentences
Using strong and weak

Name

Date

■ Look at each picture and say each sentence aloud.
  Then trace the sentences below.

 The strong lion stands.

 The lion is strong.

The lion is strong.

The lion is strong.

 The lion is weak.

The lion is weak.

The lion is weak.

■ Look at each picture and say each sentence aloud.
   Then trace and write the sentences below.

The tiger is strong.

The tiger is weak.

The monkey is strong.

The monkey is weak.

Name

Date

■ Look at each picture and say each sentence aloud.
   Then write the sentences below.

The truck is slow.

The truck is fast.

The zebra is slow.

The zebra is fast.

The tea is hot.

The tea is cold.

■ Look at each picture and say each sentence aloud.
  Then write the sentences below.

The soup is hot.

The soup is cold.

The tiger is strong.

The tiger is weak.

The monkey is strong.

The monkey is weak.

26 Practicing Adjectives
Using red, blue, wet and dry

Name	
Date	

■ Read the adjectives aloud. Trace them below.
   Then trace the sentences as you look at each picture.

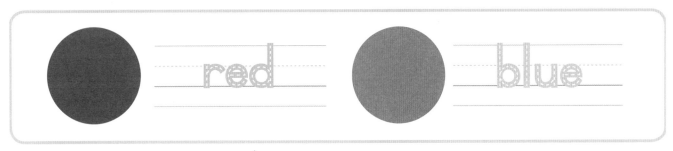

red   blue

The red towel is wet.

The red towel is wet.

The red towel is wet.

The blue towel is dry.

The blue towel is dry.

The blue towel is dry.

Using red, blue, wet and dry

■ Look at each picture and say each sentence aloud.
  Then trace and write the sentences below.

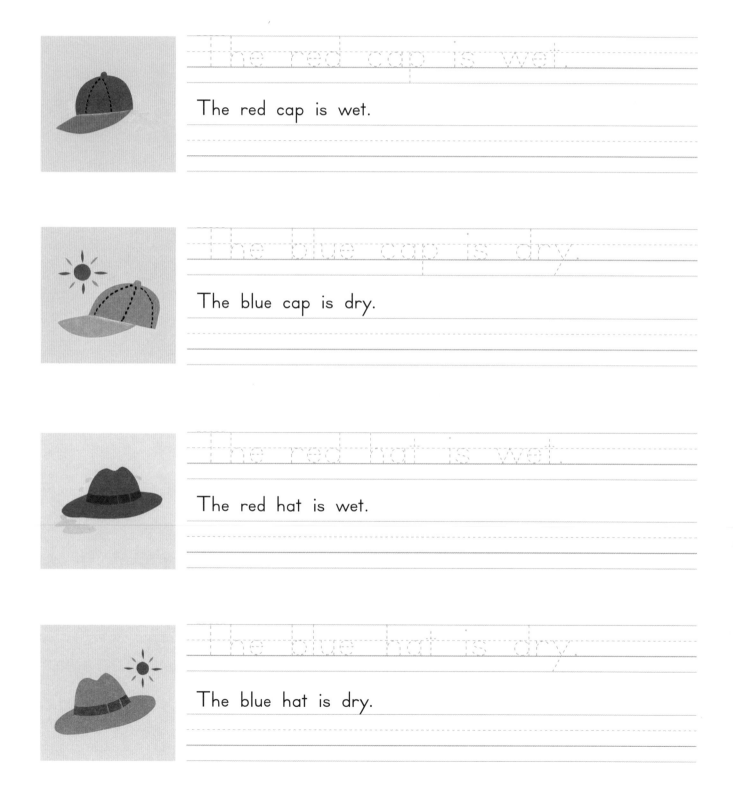

The red cap is wet.

The blue cap is dry.

The red hat is wet.

The blue hat is dry.

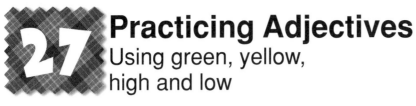

Practicing Adjectives
Using green, yellow, high and low

Name

Date

■ Read the adjectives aloud. Trace them below.
  Then trace the sentences as you look at each picture.

green   yellow

The green tower is high.

The green tower is high.

The green tower is high.

The yellow tower is low.

The yellow tower is low.

The yellow tower is low.

■ Look at each picture and say each sentence aloud.
  Then trace and write the sentences below.

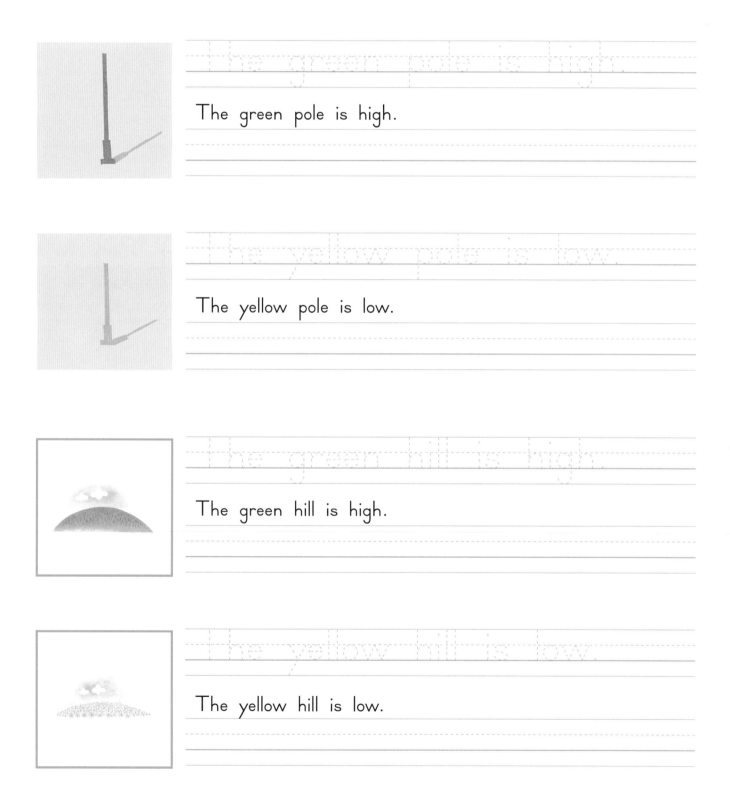

The green pole is high.

The yellow pole is low.

The green hill is high.

The yellow hill is low.

Practicing Adjectives
Using silver, gold,
narrow and wide

Name

Date

■ Read the adjectives aloud. Trace them below.
  Then trace the sentences as you look at each picture.

silver   gold

The silver door is wide.

The silver door is wide.

The silver door is wide.

The gold door is narrow.

The gold door is narrow.

The gold door is narrow.

■ Look at each picture and say each sentence aloud.
   Then trace and write the sentences below.

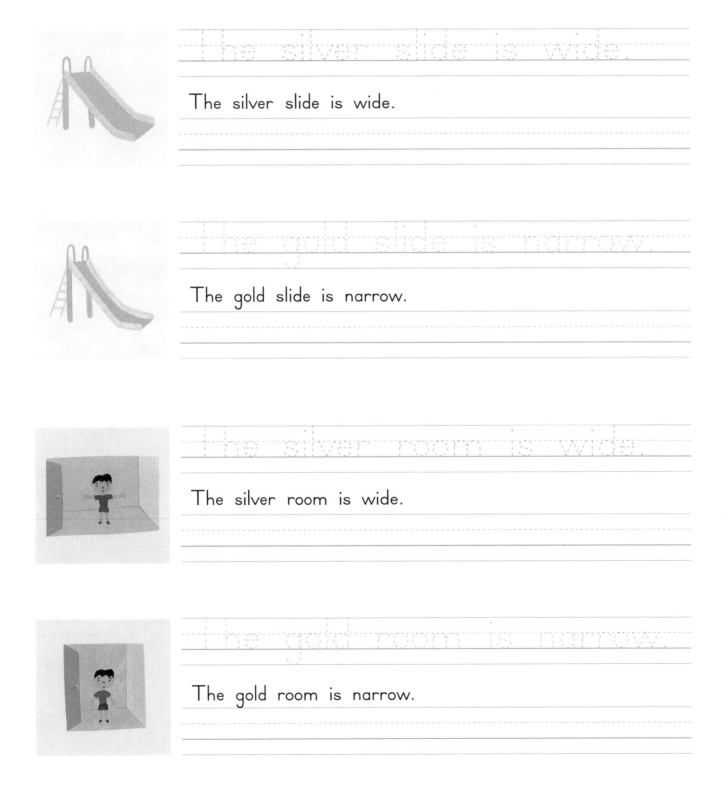

The silver slide is wide.

The silver slide is wide.

The gold slide is narrow.

The gold slide is narrow.

The silver room is wide.

The silver room is wide.

The gold room is narrow.

The gold room is narrow.

Name

Date

■ Look at each picture and say each sentence aloud.
  Then write the sentences below.

The red cap is wet.

The blue cap is dry.

The red hat is wet.

The blue hat is dry.

The green pole is high.

The yellow pole is low.

■ Look at each picture and say each sentence aloud.
  Then write the sentences below.

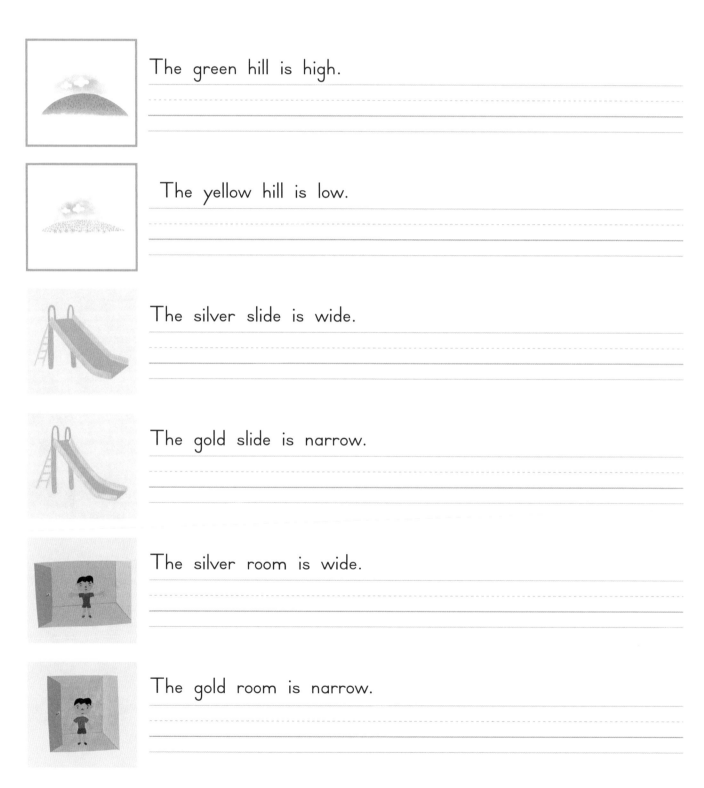

The green hill is high.

The yellow hill is low.

The silver slide is wide.

The gold slide is narrow.

The silver room is wide.

The gold room is narrow.

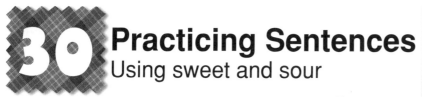

30 Practicing Sentences
Using sweet and sour

Name

Date

To parents
In this section, your child will practice using the plural form of 'to be.' If your child is having difficulty, try pointing out that the examples in the exercises are plural.

■ Look at each picture and say each sentence aloud.
   Then trace the sentences below.

 The drink is sweet.

The drinks are sweet.

The drinks are sweet.

The drinks are sweet.

The drinks are sour.

The drinks are sour.

The drinks are sour.

■ Look at each picture and say each sentence aloud.
   Then trace and write the sentences below.

The apples are sweet.

The apples are sour.

The grapes are sweet.

The grapes are sour.

Name

Date

■ Look at each picture and say each sentence aloud.
  Then trace the sentences below.

The bed is soft.

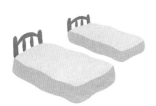

The beds are soft.

The beds are soft.

The beds are soft.

The beds are hard.

The beds are hard.

The beds are hard.

■ Look at each picture and say each sentence aloud.
  Then trace and write the sentences below.

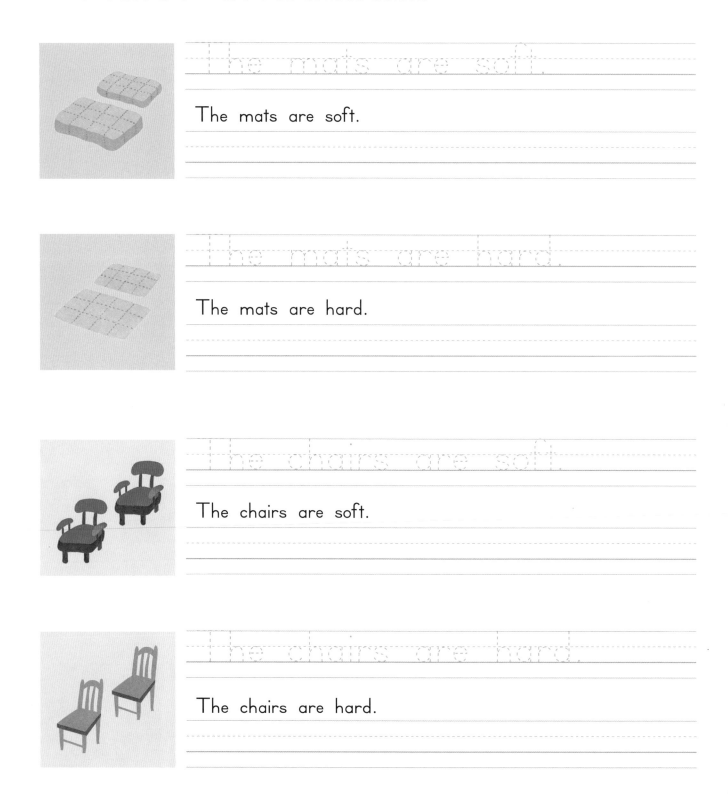

The mats are soft.

The mats are hard.

The chairs are soft.

The chairs are hard.

32 Practicing Sentences
Using full and empty

Name

Date

■ Look at each picture and say each sentence aloud.
Then trace the sentences below.

The cup is full.

The cups are full.

The cups are full.

The cups are full.

The cups are empty.

The cups are empty.

The cups are empty.

■ Look at each picture and say each sentence aloud.
  Then trace and write the sentences below.

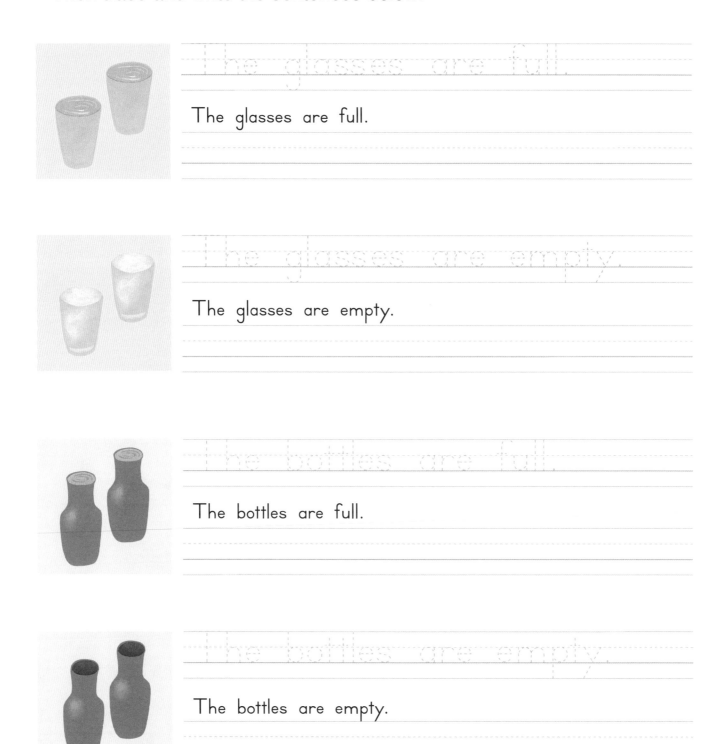

The glasses are full.

The glasses are empty.

The bottles are full.

The bottles are empty.

33 Review
Using adjectives

■ Look at each picture and say each sentence aloud.
  Then write the sentences below.

The apples are sweet.

The apples are sour.

The grapes are sweet.

The grapes are sour.

The mats are soft.

The mats are hard.

■ Look at each picture and say each sentence aloud.
   Then write the sentences below.

The chairs are soft.

The chairs are hard.

The glasses are full.

The glasses are empty.

The bottles are full.

The bottles are empty.

34 Practicing Adjectives
Using fast, faster and fastest

Name

Date

■ Read the adjectives aloud. Trace and write them below.
Then write the sentences as you look at each picture.

fast	faster	fastest
fast	faster	fastest

The runner is fast.

The bike is faster.

The car is the fastest.

■ Look at each picture and say each sentence aloud.
   Then write the sentences below.

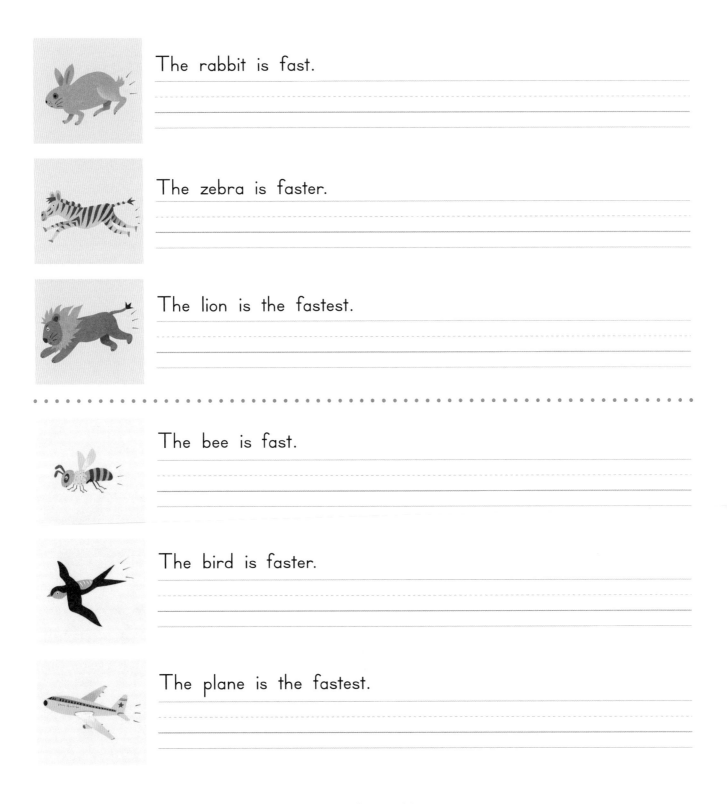

The rabbit is fast.

The zebra is faster.

The lion is the fastest.

The bee is fast.

The bird is faster.

The plane is the fastest.

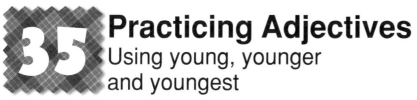

Practicing Adjectives
Using young, younger and youngest

■ Read the adjectives aloud. Trace and write them below.
 Then write the sentences as you look at each picture.

young	younger	youngest
young	younger	youngest

The man is young.

The boy is younger.

The baby is the youngest.

■ Look at each picture and say each sentence aloud.
Then write the sentences below.

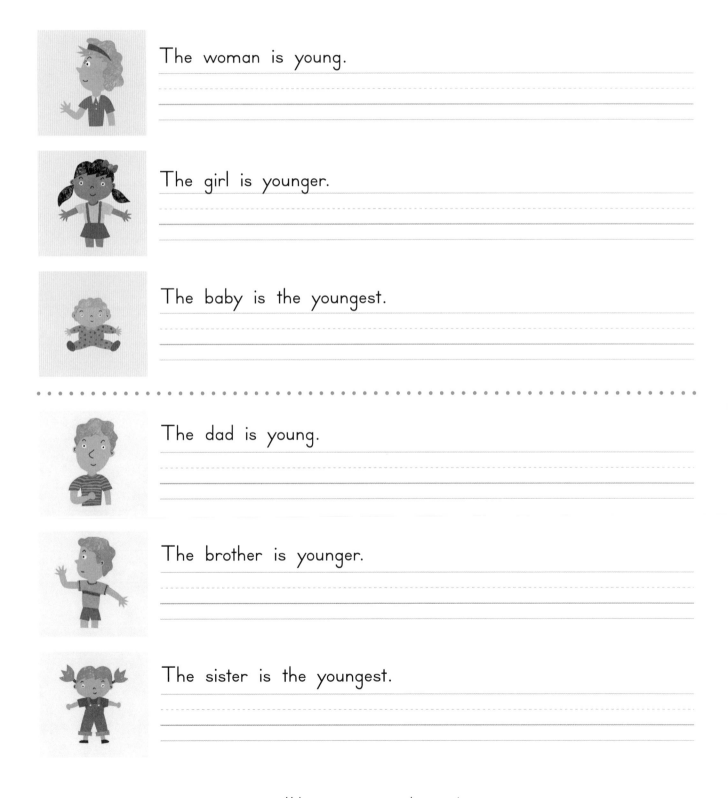

The woman is young.

The girl is younger.

The baby is the youngest.

The dad is young.

The brother is younger.

The sister is the youngest.

36 Practicing Adjectives
Using big, bigger and biggest

Name

Date

■ Read the adjectives aloud. Trace and write them below.
Then write the sentences as you look at each picture.

big	bigger	biggest
big	bigger	biggest

The bus is big.

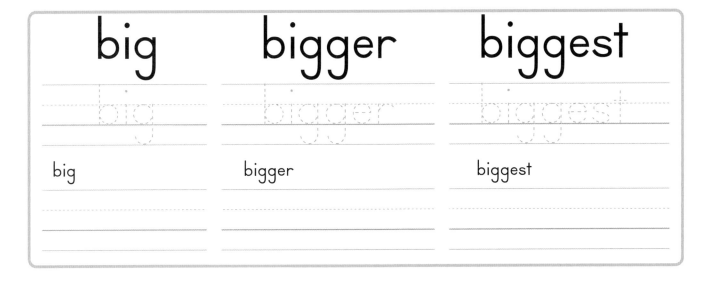

The truck is bigger.

The train is the biggest.

■ Look at each picture and say each sentence aloud.
  Then write the sentences below.

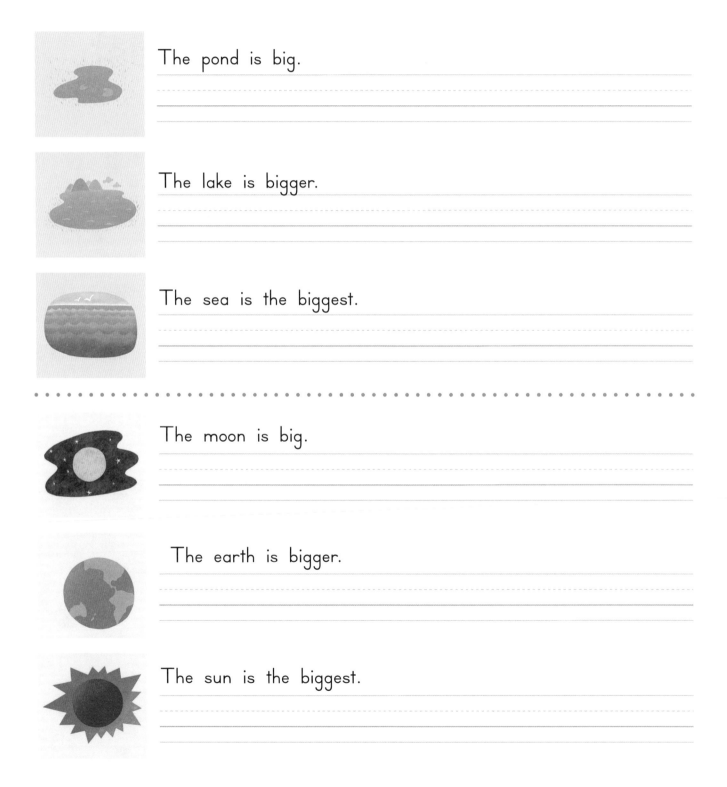

The pond is big.

The lake is bigger.

The sea is the biggest.

The moon is big.

The earth is bigger.

The sun is the biggest.

Review
Using adjectives to compare objects

■ Look at each picture and say each sentence aloud.
  Then write the sentences below.

The rabbit is fast.

The zebra is faster.

The lion is the fastest.

The woman is young.

The girl is younger.

The baby is the youngest.

■ Look at each picture and say each sentence aloud.
  Then write the sentences below.

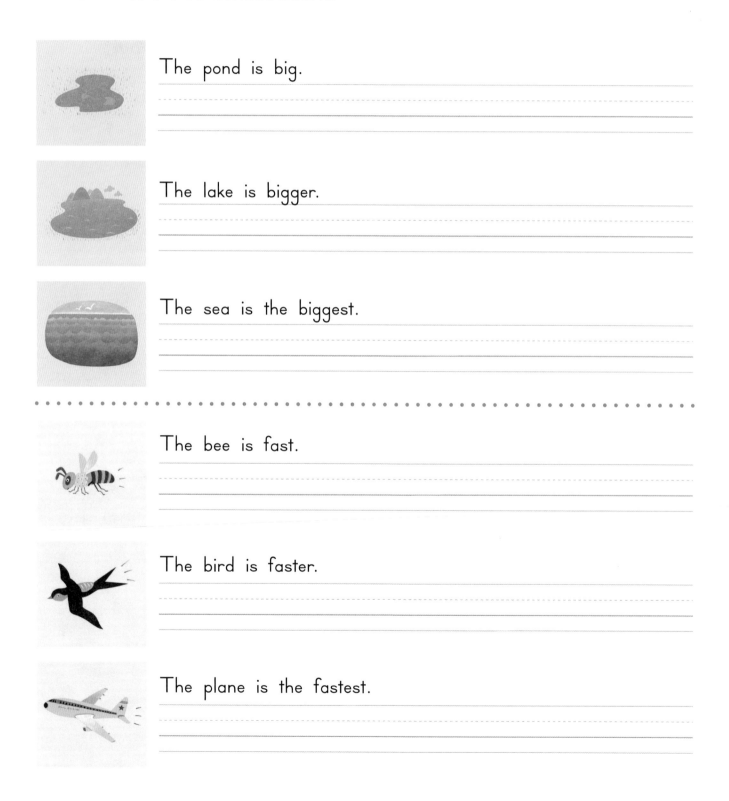

The pond is big.

The lake is bigger.

The sea is the biggest.

The bee is fast.

The bird is faster.

The plane is the fastest.

Name

Date

■ Look at each picture and say each sentence aloud.
  Then write the sentences below.

 The bear is big.

 The bear is small.

 The doll is new.

 The doll is old.

 The ham is thin.

 The ham is thick.

■ Look at each picture and say each sentence aloud.
Then write the sentences below.

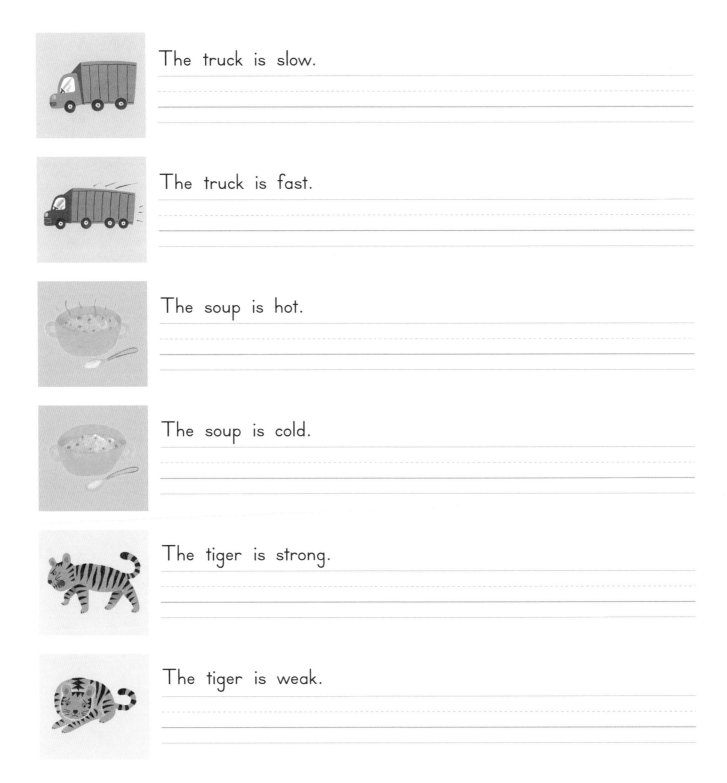

The truck is slow.

The truck is fast.

The soup is hot.

The soup is cold.

The tiger is strong.

The tiger is weak.

Review
Using adjectives

■ Look at each picture and say each sentence aloud.
  Then write the sentences below.

 The red cap is wet.

_____

_____

 The blue cap is dry.

_____

_____

 The silver slide is wide.

_____

_____

 The gold slide is narrow.

_____

_____

 The green hill is high.

_____

_____

 The yellow hill is low.

_____

_____

■ Look at each picture and say each sentence aloud.
Then write the sentences below.

The apples are sweet.

The apples are sour.

The chairs are soft.

The chairs are hard.

The bottles are full.

The bottles are empty.

Review
Using adjectives to compare objects

To parents
Has your child enjoyed learning how to use adjectives to make more complicated sentences? He or she has become familiar with a new part of speech. Please give your child lots of praise.

■ Look at each picture and say each sentence aloud.
   Then write the sentences below.

The dad is young.

The brother is younger.

The sister is the youngest.

The moon is big.

The earth is bigger.

The sun is the biggest.

■ Look at each picture and say each sentence aloud.
  Then write the sentences below.

The runner is fast.

The bike is faster.

The car is the fastest.

· ·

The bus is big.

The truck is bigger.

The train is the biggest.

KUM○N

Certificate of Achievement

is hereby congratulated on completing

My Book of Sentences

Presented on _____ _____, 20____

_____
Parent or Guardian